What Some People Will Do

Jeanie Stewart
Illustrated by Elizabeth Buttler

STECK-VAUGHN
Harcourt Supplemental Publishers

www.steck-vaughn.com

ISBN 0-7398-7535-3

Copyright © 2004 Steck-Vaughn, a division of Harcourt Supplemental Publishers, Inc. All rights reserved. No part of the material protected by this copyright may be reproduced or utilized in any form or by any means, electronic or mechanical, including photocopying, recording, or by any information storage and retrieval system, without permission in writing from the copyright owner. Requests for permission to make copies of any part of the work should be mailed to: Copyright Permissions, Steck-Vaughn, P.O. Box 26015, Austin, Texas 78755.

Power Up! Building Reading Strength is a trademark of Steck-Vaughn.

Printed in China.

1 2 3 4 5 6 7 8 9 M 07 06 05 04 03

Contents

Chapter 1
Nina the Invisible 1

Chapter 2
The Book Hunt 11

Chapter 3
A Bad Hair Day 21

Chapter 4
Real Computer Detectives 31

Chapter 5
Mystery Solved 39

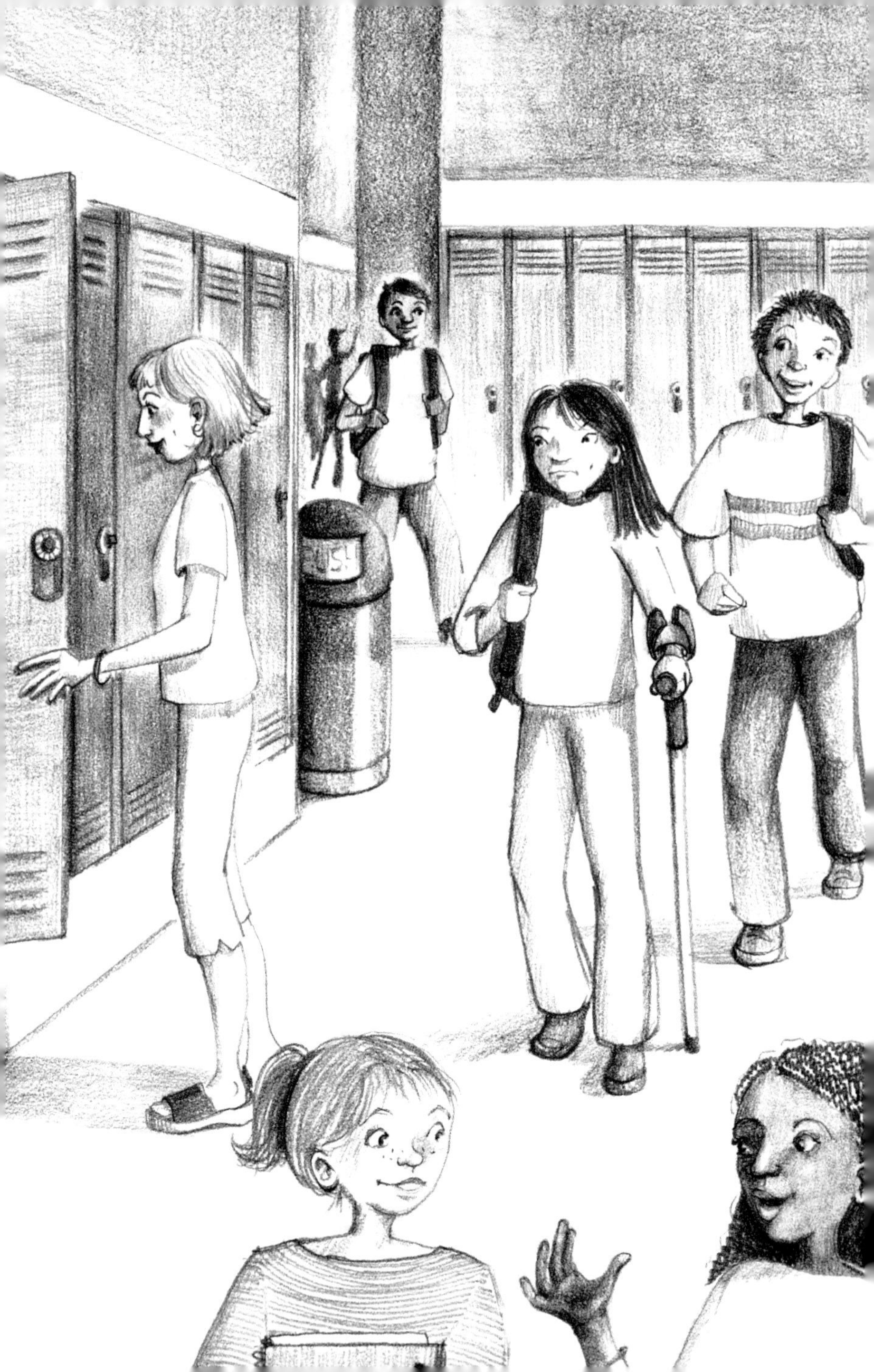

Chapter 1

Nina the Invisible

On my first day of eighth grade, I learned a tough lesson. I learned that everyone in my class had gotten taller, smarter, or prettier over the summer. Everyone had changed—except me. I was still just plain Nina Song.

The tallest and prettiest of all was Rowena Flores, who had moved to town a few months before. Nobody noticed me when Rowena was around. I felt invisible all day.

At least Koby Carter remembered that we were supposed to walk home together. Koby is my neighbor and the boy I like. I think he likes me, too, but some days I'm not sure. I was so glad to see him after school that I forgot my bad mood and smiled.

1

"What are you smiling about?" he asked.

I couldn't tell him that he was the reason, of course. "I was thinking about all the fun we'll have at the back-to-school dance on Saturday," I said. Then I paused to give him time to ask me to go to the dance with him.

Koby wasn't thinking about the dance, though. "I can't believe that Mrs. Wolf really assigned a book report on the first day of school," he grumbled. "I read enough books over the summer."

Koby's parents had assigned him ten book reports at the beginning of the summer. At first Koby had tried to fake them, but he always got caught. Finally he had found the *Computer Detective* mysteries and read ten of them.

On our way outside, Koby and I walked by the school library. I got an idea. "Why don't we start on our report now?" I asked. "Then we'll get it over with sooner."

Koby shrugged and walked inside with me. He went straight to the *Computer Detective* mysteries and picked up book number ten.

"You've already read that one," I told him.

"Mrs. Wolf doesn't know that," he said.

"Koby," I warned. "Don't start faking book reports again."

He winked at me. "I won't be faking. I really read it."

I took the book from him and put it back on the shelf. "Get a new book," I said.

"Okay, I'll see whether they have number eleven," Koby said. "It just came out. Rose Pryor, the writer, was talking about it on TV last night. She's the best writer ever."

Koby's best friend Bud shuffled over to us. "I thought I saw you two come in here," Bud said. "What's going on?"

"We're just getting a book for Mrs. Wolf's class," Koby said.

"Why bother, man?" Bud asked. He always called everyone *man*. "Just give her one of the reports you did for your parents."

Koby gave me a look, but I shook my head.

"Come on, a bunch of us are on our way to Moo's," Bud said. "You've got to come." Moo's is our favorite ice-cream shop.

Koby sighed. "Let me find a book first," he said, looking at a shelf.

"Oh, all right," said Bud. He leaned against a wall, crossing his arms. "Maybe Mario will save our table."

I heard the door open and turned my head. Then I smiled. "I don't see how," I said to Bud. "Mario just walked in."

Bud straightened up and waved Mario over. "I thought you were going to Moo's," he said.

"I am," Mario replied. "Suzy is meeting us there, too. I just have to get a gardening book for my mom first." He gave Koby a friendly whack on the arm. "Are you looking for the kids' books, Koby?"

Koby rubbed his arm. "That's very funny."

"I'm a funny guy," Mario kidded. "Am I right or what, Bud?"

Bud didn't answer. He was looking past Mario with a dreamy look on his face.

"What a surprise!" a voice said.

I groaned. It was Rowena. I could feel myself becoming invisible again.

Rowena came toward us, brushing her hair with her fingers. "I didn't know you'd be at the library, Mario," she said.

Right. She had probably been following him. Rowena had a huge crush on Mario. Mario quit smiling when he saw her, though.

"I'd better get that gardening book," he said, looking down and walking away.

"How funny! I'm here to pick up a book on gardening, too," Rowena said, following him.

"Isn't she perfect?" Bud asked with a sigh.

This was too much. Early in the summer, Koby had been crazy about Rowena, and now Bud had fallen for her. I couldn't figure out why. Rowena was a fake and a flirt.

Koby grabbed Bud by the sleeve and pulled him closer. "Watch out for Rowena," warned Koby. "She's only interested in Mario. She'll use you to get close to him."

Koby knew what he was talking about. That's exactly what Rowena had done to him at the beginning of the summer. Bud didn't look convinced, though.

Soon Mario returned with Rowena right beside him. He held up a book. "I got one," he said. "Let's go."

Rowena dropped her notebook on the floor in front of Mario. Papers flew everywhere. She fluttered her eyelashes at Mario, but he looked away. Bud bent down and helped Rowena pick up her papers.

Rowena frowned at Mario and then smiled at Bud. "Are you guys leaving?" she asked.

"Not if you don't want us to," Bud said.

Koby gave Bud a funny look. "I thought you were in a hurry to get to Moo's," he said.

Rowena's smile got wider. "Oh, I love the shakes at Moo's!"

Bud's voice squeaked as he asked, "Why don't you come with us?"

"Okay," Rowena said. "I will." She turned and followed Mario out the door.

Bud leaned toward Koby and me. He gave us a silly grin. "I think Rowena likes me," he whispered. Then he hurried to catch up with her and Mario.

When the three of them had left, I picked up a small piece of paper that Rowena and Bud had missed. *Rowena + Mario* was written all over it in purple ink.

I showed Koby the paper. "I think Bud is in big trouble," I said.

Koby agreed. "I'd better go with them to make sure that he doesn't do something really stupid—like ask Rowena to come to the dance with us."

Before Koby left the library, he turned back to look at me. "Oh, do you want to go?"

For a second I thought he was asking me to the dance. Then I realized he was talking about going to Moo's.

"No, thanks," I said with a sigh. It was nice of Koby to be polite, but he probably didn't really want me tagging along. I was Nina the Invisible again.

Chapter 2

The Book Hunt

On Friday, Mrs. Wolf sent our class to the school library to get books for our reports. After I found a book, I looked for Koby. He was sitting on the floor, searching through a low shelf. Bud was sitting at a table nearby, looking at a car magazine.

I tapped Bud's shoulder. "Mrs. Wolf is going to be mad if you don't get a book."

"Koby is finding one for me," he said.

I noticed that he kept peeking over the top of the magazine. He was looking at Mario, Suzy, and Rowena talking at a table across from him. When I asked Bud whether he'd had fun at Moo's, he just shrugged.

Koby stood up. "Bud didn't have a very good time. Rowena didn't pay any attention to him," he said.

"You're wrong, man," said Bud. "She paid attention to me after Mario left with Suzy."

"I think Mario has a crush on Suzy," Koby whispered as he handed Bud a book.

Bud looked at the title and pushed the book back at Koby. "No, thanks," he said. "I don't want a dumb *Computer Detective* mystery."

Mario shuffled over to our table and looked over Bud's shoulder at the book. "I'll take it," he said, picking up the book. "Suzy told me that these books are really simple."

"They're interesting, too," Koby said.

Bud shook his head. "They're so fake! Kids can't solve mysteries by using a computer."

"I'll bet I could," Koby said.

"Me, too," I added. "You can discover all kinds of things on the Internet."

"Maybe so, but when do real kids ever have a mystery to solve?" Bud said.

As usual, Rowena walked over and stood beside Mario. She didn't seem to care that we were talking. She started talking all about the dance and what fun it would be to decorate the gym the next day.

I sat down at Bud's table and opened my book. Mario pulled out the chair across from me. He waved to Suzy, who joined us. Rowena didn't like being ignored, so she pulled up a chair, too.

"I'm going to go ask Ms. Johnson to help me find the newest *Computer Detective* book," Koby said. He walked over to the school librarian.

Everyone was quiet for a minute. Then Rowena cleared her throat loudly. "The dance is tomorrow night. I wonder who I should go with," she said.

Bud got that dreamy look on his face again. I think he was gathering up the courage to ask Rowena to come to the dance with all of us.

Just then Koby came back. "Ms. Johnson said that she wants us to be quieter," he said. He handed Bud another *Computer Detective* book. This time, Bud was too busy looking at Rowena to argue.

Koby sat down next to me. "That's the only other *Computer Detective* book in the library," he said. "All the rest are out."

"Do you want this one back?" Mario asked, pointing to his *Computer Detective* book. "You can have it."

"No," Koby said. "I want number eleven. The library doesn't have it yet."

Rowena yawned. "I'm tired of hearing about *Computer Detective* books," she said.

"You should try one," Koby said. "They're all about this boy named Vince who uses the Internet to solve mysteries."

"I know," she said flatly. "I've read them."

"Oh, really?" I said. I didn't believe her. I'd never seen Rowena reading anything thicker than a magazine. Even then, she only looked at the pictures.

"Yes, really," Rowena said. She took the book from Bud and flipped through a few pages. "I've read all of them."

"I bet you have," I mumbled. Nobody seemed to hear me.

"Then you probably want number eleven, too," Koby said.

Rowena ran her finger down the back of the book. The back had a few words about the author printed on it. "No," she said, pretending to hold back another yawn. "I read number eleven ages ago."

"It just came out this week," I said.

Rowena smiled at me, but it wasn't a pretty smile. "I guess I got it early."

Mario started laughing. "Good joke, Ro. We almost believed you." He poked Suzy with his elbow, and she giggled.

Rowena's cheeks turned red. "I did get the book early," she said. "I know the author."

Koby's eyes got big. "Do you really know Rose Pryor?" he asked.

Rowena frowned at Suzy and Mario. "Of course I know her," she said loudly enough for everyone to hear. "Rose Pryor is my aunt."

"That's cool," Bud said. "Hey, can you get us her autograph?"

"I know what would be better," Mario said. "How about getting us an autographed book?"

Rowena closed the book and gave it back to Bud. "Is tomorrow soon enough?" she asked with a smile. "Aunt Rosa signed book number eleven for me the last time she visited."

"Don't you mean *Rose?*" I asked, narrowing my eyes. I knew I sounded mean, but Rowena was lying. Why couldn't anyone else see it?

Rowena glared at me. "Rose is the name she uses as an author. Her real name is Rosa."

I'd had enough. "I don't believe you, Rowena," I said.

I thought she would storm off, but she didn't. Instead, she started telling a big story about going to New York with her famous aunt. She had everyone's attention at last.

Before long, other students had gathered around our table. Even the librarian came over. Instead of telling Rowena that she was being too noisy, Ms. Johnson asked questions about Rose Pryor. She was just as impressed as the students were. Rowena had everyone fooled.

I just couldn't sit there and listen to Rowena anymore. I had better things to do. As I stood up to leave, I bumped Koby's chair. He looked at me with surprise.

"Nina, I didn't know you were still here," he said. "I thought you'd gone back to class."

I was invisible again.

The bell rang to go home. I left the library slowly in case Koby tried to catch up with me, but he didn't. I walked home alone, wondering how long everyone would sit there listening to Rowena's tall tales.

"I'm home!" I called to my dad. I tossed my books into a chair and locked myself in the bathroom. For a long time, I stared at myself in the mirror above the sink.

What was wrong with me? What was so special about Rowena? Was it her eyes? Was it her clothes? Was it the way she had her hair cut? Would boys be impressed if I looked more like Rowena?

I picked up a pair of scissors. Maybe other eighth graders would stop ignoring me if I had a new haircut.

Chapter 3

A Bad Hair Day

When I woke up on Saturday morning, I was hoping that my haircut had been a bad dream. It wasn't.

What looked cute on Rowena just looked horrible on me. My hair looked as though it had gotten caught in a fan. I tried brushing it back. I tried brushing it forward. I tried curling it. I even tried covering it with a hat. Nothing helped.

My dad called a woman at the beauty shop to ask if she could help. She said she could but not until late afternoon. I was stuck with the world's worst hair until then. At least it would be fixed before the dance that night.

I couldn't let bad hair stop me right now. I had to go to the school to help decorate the gym for the dance. When I got to the gym, the first person who saw me was Rowena. She was blowing up balloons at a table and called me over. She pushed some balloons toward me and started talking as if we were best friends. She didn't even mention my hair.

"Isn't it funny how much the boys are interested in the *Computer Detective* books?" she asked. "You've read them, right?"

"I read the first one," I replied.

She blew into a red balloon. When it got big, she knotted its end. "Hmm," she said. "It's been ages since I read the first one. Tell me, how did Vance solve that mystery again?"

"Don't you mean *Vince?*" I asked.

"That's what I said—Vince." She rolled her eyes and picked up another balloon.

I didn't feel like arguing, so I blew into a balloon. It popped out of my mouth and flew across the table. I sighed. Rowena even blew up balloons better than I did.

"Which of the *Computer Detective* books do you think is the most interesting one, Nina?" she asked.

"Stop it!" I said. "I know what you're doing. It won't work." She was trying to get facts from me about the *Computer Detective* books. Then she could talk about them as though she'd read them. Koby had done the same thing to me during the summer when he had tried to fake a book report.

Rowena smiled, but not at me. She was looking at Koby, who had just arrived. I knew he was going to tease me about my hair.

"Hi, Rowena," Koby said. Then he looked over at me. Suddenly he started coughing.

"Sorry," he said when he caught his breath. "I swallowed my gum."

Had he noticed my hair? I couldn't tell. I cleared my throat and asked why he was late.

"I had to go shopping. I bought a blue shirt to wear to the dance," he said.

I grinned. "Blue is my favorite color. I got a new dress. It's blue, too."

This was another perfect chance for him to ask me to the dance. I waited for him to say something, but he just looked away. I grabbed another balloon and tried to look busy.

"Let me help," Koby said, picking up a balloon and sitting down. He was filling it up with air when Bud jogged over to us and sat down across from Koby.

Bud looked at me strangely and gasped. "What's up with your—ow!" Bud jumped back and glared at Koby. "Watch it! You kicked me."

Koby glared right back at Bud. "Was that your leg?" he asked. "I thought it was the table." He finished filling his balloon and tied it.

"Boys!" Rowena scolded. If she was trying to draw their attention back to her, it worked.

"When do we get our autographed books?" Koby asked.

"You'll get them later, Koby," Rowena said. "Why don't you three finish blowing up these balloons? I think Mario needs my help setting up chairs." She quickly trotted away to where Mario and some other people were working. She was such a flirt.

Bud looked at Koby and me. "I'd better help them," he said. Then he ran after Rowena.

Koby and I stared at each other over the pile of balloons. "Can I ask you something?" he said at last. I held my breath. Was he finally going to ask me to the dance?

Koby leaned closer. "Why are you being so mean to Rowena?" I was so surprised by his question that I didn't know what to say.

"You're usually nice to everyone," he continued. "It's not like you to be so mean."

"I have a bigger question," I said angrily. "Why are *you* being so nice to her, Koby? Don't you remember how she walked out on you when you invited her to watch movies at my apartment?"

Koby rolled his eyes. "Sure I remember, but she had just moved here. It's hard to be the new kid. Just give her a chance, Nina. Don't forget—her aunt's a very famous writer."

I wasn't convinced that her aunt was famous. I said I'd try to be nicer to Rowena, though. Then Koby looked over at her. "Hey, she's giving Mario a book."

The two of us walked across the gym to where Mario was holding *Computer Detective* number eleven.

"That's the one I wanted," said Koby.

"Sorry," Rowena said. "I only had that one book at home." She smiled sweetly. "Don't worry, though. I called my aunt in Jackson, Mississippi. She'll send more autographed books next week."

"Look," Mario said. "It really is signed by Rose Pryor!" He held the book open so that everyone could see.

"Let me see that!" I said. I took the book from Mario and looked more closely. Some of the letters looked very familiar. The *R*'s at the beginning and end of the words *Rose Pryor* looked just like the *R*'s I'd seen written all over Rowena's note paper.

Rowena took the book from me. "That belongs to Mario," she said in a nasty voice. "You'll have to wait for your own book."

I wanted to accuse Rowena of signing the book herself, but who'd believe me? Everyone loved Rowena and believed her story.

A photographer from the school newspaper came over to us. "Hold still!" she said. "Let me get a picture of all of you."

"Wait!" Rowena said. She gave me a little push. "Nina, would you go over there and get my purse? I need my lipstick."

I glared at her, but Bud stepped in. "I'll get it for you," he said.

"No, let Nina," Rowena said, patting her hair and smiling for the camera. "She doesn't really want to be in the picture anyway, not with *that* hair."

I looked at her with my mouth open, but I didn't know what to say. Someone had finally said something about my hair. Why did that person have to be Rowena? This time, I really wanted to be invisible.

Chapter 4

Real Computer Detectives

With everyone watching, what could I do? I walked over to the balloon table and grabbed Rowena's purse. I didn't notice that it was open until stuff fell out all over the table.

There was a pencil, a brush, and a tube of lipstick. There was also another piece of paper with *Rowena + Mario* written on it. Rowena had probably filled up a whole notebook with those words.

"What's taking you so long?" Koby asked.

I jumped. I hadn't heard him follow me over to the table. I quickly put things back into Rowena's purse.

Koby picked up a piece of paper and handed it to me. "You missed this," he said.

I looked at the paper. It was from Brown's, a big bookstore downtown. The paper was a receipt for the sale of one *Computer Detective* book. I took a deep breath and looked again to make sure I wasn't wrong.

I showed Koby the receipt. "I think that Rowena bought Mario's *Computer Detective* book this morning," I said quietly.

Koby looked at it and scratched his head. "What about the autograph?"

"I think Rowena wrote it herself," I said. I showed Koby the piece of paper with *Rowena + Mario* written on it. "You saw the autograph in Mario's book. What do you think?"

Koby paused for a moment, and then he frowned. "I think you're right," he said. He put the piece of paper in his pocket. "Should we go tell the others?"

I looked across the gym at Rowena. People were standing around her, and she was smiling for the photographer. She hadn't bothered to wait for her lipstick.

"No one will believe us," I said sadly. "We don't have enough proof."

Koby suddenly cheered up. "Then let's go to the library to find proof," he said with a big smile. "We'll be *real* computer detectives."

"Okay," I said. I left Rowena's purse on the table. She could get it herself.

Later, when Koby and I got back to the gym, all the decorations were up. Only a few students were there, but Rowena was still the center of attention.

33

Suzy was interviewing Rowena for the school paper. Bud and Mario stood nearby, watching them. Koby and I headed over to the group and listened.

"Where did you say your aunt lived?" Suzy asked Rowena.

Rowena sighed as if she were getting tired of answering questions about her aunt. "She lives in Mississippi," she said. "I just love to visit her there. I travel a lot, you know. Do you want to hear about the places I've been?"

"Um, maybe some other time," Suzy said. "Okay, here's my last question. How long has your aunt been writing?"

Rowena rolled her eyes and frowned. "How should I know? She's old. I guess she's been writing a long time."

I could tell that Rowena was getting a bit impatient. Was it because Suzy wasn't letting her talk about herself? Maybe it was because Mario was standing near Suzy.

A few minutes later, Suzy put away her notes. She thanked Rowena and then took Mario's hand. They turned toward us.

Bud looked excited. "Tell Nina and Koby the good news," he said.

"Tomorrow my dad is going to interview Rowena about her aunt," Suzy said. Her dad interviewed people on a TV talk show every Sunday morning.

"I don't think that's a good idea," I said. I told them about finding the receipt from the bookstore in Rowena's purse. "Rowena just bought the book and signed Rose Pryor's name," I said.

Koby handed Mario the piece of paper I'd given him. "Compare the autograph in your book to this writing," Koby said. "The writing slants a different way, but the *R*'s are the same. See how they curl?"

Rowena stood a few feet away from us. I knew she was listening.

While Mario was comparing the names, Bud leaned closer so that he could see them, too. "Lots of people make curly *R*'s, man," he said. "You don't have real proof."

"I thought you might say that, Bud," I said. "That's why Koby and I went to the library. We found some interesting facts on the Internet about Rose Pryor." I turned to Koby. "Tell everyone what we found out."

"You know, Rowena has said many times that her aunt is from Mississippi," said Koby.

Suzy held up her notes. "I've got it written down right here."

Rowena marched up to Koby. "Don't accuse me of lying. My aunt Rose *is* from Mississippi. Just read the back of this *Computer Detective* book!" She grabbed the book from Mario and read out loud from the back cover. "Rose Pryor lives in Jackson with her dog, Buffy," she read, giving me a nasty look.

Koby cleared his throat. "Since Rowena is from Mississippi, it was easy for her to think that the book meant Jackson, Mississippi," he said. "I learned by checking Rose Pryor's Web site that the author is from Jackson, *Missouri*. Look at this page I printed out."

Suzy looked at the page and frowned. "I'd think you'd know what state your own aunt is from," she said to Rowena.

"That's not all we found," I said. "There was an interview with Ms. Pryor on her web site. She said that she started writing because she was a lonely child. She didn't have any brothers or sisters to play with."

I looked right at Rowena. "In the interview she also said that she's never been married. If she isn't married and never had a brother or sister, she couldn't be anyone's aunt."

No one said anything. We all just stared at Rowena. She stared back for a second. Then she dropped the book and ran to the bathroom.

Chapter 5

Mystery Solved

I'm not sure why I hurried after Rowena, but I did. Maybe it was because I felt so sorry for her. I stepped into the bathroom. I could hear her crying inside one of the stalls.

"Rowena, please come out of there," I said, knocking on the stall door.

"No!" she said, sniffing loudly.

"Will you tell me why you lied to us?" I asked gently. "You didn't have to."

I heard a click, and the door swung open. Rowena's eyes were red.

"Do you know that I lived in three different towns last year?" she asked. "My family moves so much. I can never make friends."

I led her to the sink and gave her a paper towel. "I just wanted everyone to like me," she continued, wiping her eyes. "I wanted Mario to ask me to the dance, but he likes Suzy. It was all for nothing." She started crying again.

It was strange, but I wasn't angry with Rowena anymore. I knew how she felt. She wanted people to pay attention to her. Maybe telling stories was her way of trying not to be invisible. I had chopped off my hair for the same reason!

I put a hand on Rowena's shoulder. "Just apologize. We'll understand."

She shook her head and pulled away. "No one will ever want to speak to me again!"

"Come on, Rowena. I think everyone will understand, if you're honest with us," I said. "Let's go."

Mario, Suzy, Bud, and Koby were waiting near the gym door. When Mario saw Rowena and me walking toward the group, he looked away. Suzy ripped up her interview notes.

No one said anything for a few seconds. Finally Rowena apologized. "I'm sorry I lied to all of you," she said. She explained that she had only been trying to make friends.

Mario gave Rowena a friendly pat on the shoulder. "We all make mistakes," he said. "Let's put them behind us for now. We'll see you tonight at the dance." He and Suzy turned and walked away.

"He'll see all of *you* tonight," Rowena said. "I'm not going." She picked up her purse and started walking toward the door.

Bud stopped her. "You're not going, after all the work you've done on these decorations? You have to go!"

Rowena shook her head sadly. "No one wants me to be at the dance."

"We do," Bud said with a smile. "Would you go with us, Rowena?"

Rowena's eyes got really wide. "Do you mean it? You really want me to go to the dance with you, after all the trouble I caused?"

Bud smiled. "Like Mario said, we all make mistakes. What do you say?"

Rowena looked as though she were going to cry again, but she held back her tears. She nodded, and then she and Bud walked out the door together.

"Well, Computer Detective, we solved the Mystery of Aunt Author," Koby kidded. "Our work is done. It's time for us to go home."

"Thanks for believing in me, Koby," I said.

"I always believe in you, Nina," he replied.

I smiled, then rubbed my chin. "There's still one big unsolved mystery, though," I said.

Koby lifted an eyebrow. "Oh, what is it?"

I couldn't wait any longer. I had to ask him. "Who are you going to the dance with? Be honest with me."

Koby looked confused. "I thought we were all going together. Besides, you know I can't dance very well."

I could feel my cheeks getting red. I took a deep breath and asked, "Would you dance with me anyway?"

He smiled. "Sure, I'll dance with you, Nina."

I let out my breath. "Well, I guess that solves all the mysteries."

"No, there's one more big mystery," Koby said. He looped his arm around my elbow.

I gave him a strange look. "What?" I asked.

"Why on earth did you do that to your hair?" He wrinkled his nose and pointed at me.

I laughed. "That's one mystery better left unsolved," I said.

I could hardly wait for the dance. Koby's shirt would match my blue dress, and we'd look so good together. It would almost be like a date! Of course, I had to get ready for a date at the beauty shop before then.

We walked outside for some fresh air. As we laughed and talked, I had a great feeling. I wasn't invisible anymore.